ANIMAL SPORTS

Jim Gigliotti

Raintree

WID.

www.raintreepublishers.co.uk
Visit our website to find out more information about Raintree books.

To order:

☎ Phone 0845 6044371

🖨 Fax +44 (0) 1865 312263

💻 Email myorders@raintreepublishers.co.uk

Customers from outside the UK please telephone +44 1865 312262

Raintree is an imprint of Capstone Global Library Limited, a company incorporated in England and Wales having its registered office at 7 Pilgrim Street, London, EC4V 6LB – Registered company number: 6695582

Edited by Rebecca Rissman, Dan Nunn, and Catherine Veitch
Designed by Joanna Hinton Malivoire
Picture research by Ruth Blair
Originated by Capstone Global Library
Printed and bound in China by CTPS

ISBN 978 1 406 22691 1 (hardback)
15 14 13 12 11
10 9 8 7 6 5 4 3 2 1

ISBN 978 1 406 22698 0 (paperback)
16 15 14 13 12
10 9 8 7 6 5 4 3 2 1

British Library Cataloguing in Publication Data
Gigliotti, Jim
Animal sports. – (Extreme sport)
798-dc22
A full catalogue record for this book is available from the British Library.

Acknowledgements
We would like to thank the following for permission to reproduce photographs: Corbis pp. 5 (© Baz Ratner/Reuters), 7 (© JOCHEN LUEBKE/epa), 12 (© Salah Ibrahim/epa), 15 (© Atlantide Phototravel), 17 (© Laurent Gillieron/epa), 22 (© JAVIER BARBANCHO/Reuters), 26 (© John Carnemolla), 29 (© Rick Gomez); Photolibrary pp. 9 (Aurora Photos/Melissa Farlow), 10 (Loop Images/Neil Tingle), 24 (Radius Images); Shutterstock pp. 4 (© Nightman1965), 6 (© Kondrashov Mlkhail Evgenevich), 8 (© Niar), 11 (© Allan Kilgour), 13 (© Jayspy), 14 (© Ventura), 16 (© Oliver Hoffmann), 18 (© Perry Correll), 19 (© JeremyRichards), 20 (© TFoxFoto), 21 (© TFoxFoto), 23 (© gary yim), 25 (© sonya etchison), 27 (© Dennis Donohue), 28 (© Vladimir Melnik).

Cover photograph of a steeplechase reproduced with permission of Photolibrary (White).

Every effort has been made to contact copyright holders of material reproduced in this book. Any omissions will be rectified in subsequent printings if notice is given to the publisher.

All the internet addresses (URLs) given in this book were valid at the time of going to press. However, due to the dynamic nature of the internet, some addresses may have changed, or sites may have changed or ceased to exist since publication. While the author and publisher regret any inconvenience this may cause readers, no responsibility for any such changes can be accepted by either the author or the publisher.

Some words are shown in bold, **like this**. You can find out what they mean by looking in the glossary.

Contents

Animals in sport

People all over the world keep pets or farm animals. But did you ever think about animals taking part in extreme sports? Athletes work with animals to jump, race, and fight in many exciting sporting events!

STAY SAFE!
Remember to stay safe in all sports. Always wear protective clothing and make sure you have adult supervision.

Best in the show

In show jumping, horses complete the twisting and curving course while jumping over fences, railings, and low walls. It's not a race. Horses need to finish in a certain amount of time, but doing it right is what counts.

WOW!

In the high jump event, horses and riders often jump over walls that are more than 2 metres tall. That's higher than a car!

Off to the races!

Unlike show jumping, horse racing is all about speed! The first horse and **jockey** to cross the finishing line wins. In **thoroughbred** racing, jockeys ride on top of the horse. In harness racing, jockeys ride behind the horse in carts called sulkies.

WOW!

Horses in thoroughbred races can run at up to 50 kilometres an hour! That's as fast as a motor scooter!

Steeple to steeple

In the steeplechase, horses run several kilometres over a course that includes fences, hedges, and water. Most steeplechase races are held in the United Kingdom and France.

WOW!

The steeplechase got its name in Ireland in the 1750s. Horses raced from church **steeple** to church steeple in different towns.

The long haul

Horses and riders cover distances of 80 kilometres or more in **endurance** riding. Just completing the race is an achievement. Rugged ground or harsh weather make endurance riding an extreme challenge.

WOW!
Endurance riding is so difficult that riders must stop at **veterinary** checkpoints to make sure the horses are okay.

Super sleds!

In sled dog racing, teams of dogs and human drivers compete on icy and snowy trails. Some race dogs can run at up to 32 kilometres per hour. That's as fast as a car drives through a town.

WOW!

Winners have taken up to 20 days to complete the Iditarod Trail Sled Dog Race in Alaska, United States.

Clever canines

In **agility** competitions dogs race through tunnels, jump over fences, and dart up and down ramps. Trainers lead the dogs along the course. They've got to be in great shape to keep up with their four-legged friends!

WOW!
In **canine** freestyle, a dog and its handler perform dance routines to music.

Polo

Polo players use a **mallet** to score goals by hitting a ball in between posts. The tricky part is that the players are on horseback! The fields are huge – three times longer than a football pitch.

WOW!

In places like India and Thailand, they play polo on elephants!

19

Cowboys and cowgirls

Cowboys used to compete among themselves to see who could do their jobs the best. That led to a new sport in the late 1800s, called the rodeo. A rodeo is made up of events such as roping, **steer** wrestling, and bull riding.

roping

bull riding

Rodeos are different from most of the other animal sports we've read about because the winner is the most skilled person, not the most skilled animal.

Olé!

In bullfighting **matadors stalk** the animal. They wave a cape to distract the bull. "Olé!" the crowd roars.

Many people think bullfighting is wrong because the bull is often killed. Others think it is okay because it is an important part of the **culture** in places such as Spain and Peru. What do you think?

Respect for animals

Bullfighting is not the only animal sport that people have complained about. Some people believe animals are unfairly treated whenever they are used for entertainment.

There are two sides to every argument, though. Trainers and athletes know it's important to respect the animals.

Staying healthy

Animals in sport have to be fit and healthy, but so do humans! Getting proper exercise and **nutrition** is the first step for everyone involved in animal sports.

Get fit!

Do you want to get into animal sports one day? You can start by getting fit! **Experts** say that children should get at least 60 to 90 minutes of exercise each day.

There are lots of ways to exercise. You can ride a bike, run, or hop. Climbing in playgrounds is great exercise. Even if you don't get involved in animal sports, you'll feel great!

Glossary

agility ability to move quickly and easily

canine to do with dogs

culture beliefs and ideas that are common in a country or group of people

endurance able to last for a long time, for example, while playing sports

expert person with a special skill or knowledge

jockey athlete who rides a horse, or other animal in competition

mallet long-handled hammer with a large head

matador man who takes part in a bullfight

nutrition food that keeps you healthy

stalk follow quietly

steeple tall tower on a building

steer bullock

thoroughbred horse bred for racing

veterinary to do with the care of animals that are ill or injured

Find out more

Books

Horsing Around: Show Jumping, Robin Johnson (Crabtree, 2009)

Horsing Around: Steeplechase, Martha Martin (Crabtree, 2009)

Learn to Ride, Carolyn Henderson (Dorling Kindersley, 2005)

Website

www.ykc.org.uk/
This is the website for the Young Kennel Club. Find out more about dog agility courses and lots of other information about dogs.

Place to visit

Loch Morlich, Cairngorm Mountains, Scotland
The Aviemore dog sled races are held over two days every January. More than 200 dog teams take part.

Index